The Spark in ME!

Shilpi Sharma

BookLeaf Publishing

India | USA | UK

Presentation by *BookLeaf Publishing*

Web: www.bookleafpub.com

E-mail: info@bookleafpub.com

ISBN:

First edition 2024

To all those girls struggling to find their voice, this book is as much yours as it is mine. May its words resonate with you, inspire you, and remind you that you are never alone in the vast expanse of existence.

ACKNOWLEDGEMENT

A big 'thank you' to my family, whose unwavering love and encouragement have been the foundation upon which I've built my dreams, thank you for believing in me even when I doubted myself.

A heartfelt thank you to all my friends, whose laughter and camaraderie have brought light into the darkest of days, thank you for being my constant companions on this rollercoaster ride called life.

PREFACE

These verses are not mere words; they are fragments of my existence woven into the fabric of time. Each poem is a snapshot, a snapshot capturing moments of joy, sorrow, love, and longing—the essence of what it means to be human.

As I pen down these lines, I am reminded of the winding paths I've traveled, the peaks I've climbed, and the valleys I've traversed. Every poem bears witness to the complexities of my journey—the triumphs and tribulations, the laughter and tears, the victories and defeats.

Through poetry, I've found solace in the chaos, clarity in the confusion, and beauty in the mundane. It is my sincerest hope that within these pages, you'll find resonance with your own experiences, that my words may serve as mirrors reflecting the myriad shades of the human heart.

I offer this collection not as a memoir, but as a testament to the power of language to transcend barriers, to heal wounds, and to connect souls across time and space. May these verses find their way into the quiet corners of your heart, stirring echoes of your own journey and illuminating the path ahead.

The Bloom

It was the summer of 2002,
I was moving away,
Elated, yet a little sad too,
With a life ahead, but having to let go of you.
I watched the days go by,
In each moment, I felt a longing rise.
I wondered if I was losing my mind,
Was it real, or just me intertwined?
I wanted to share it all with you,
But too scared to reach out, unsure what to do.
Worried that I was already history,
I took the first step to end my misery.
Back then, it was Internet cafes that were the
way,
And one day, I walked into one, hoping for a
sign.
A smile spread across my face,
When I saw your name in an email, so fine.

I'd never known such joy,
A feeling that turned my world into a magical
place.
Amidst the loneliness, in that foreign land,
I could feel my heart bloom, your love within
my embrace.

Across the Miles

Eighteen, and my heart learns to ache,
Not from pain, but the space we can't break.
You, my best friend, now something more,
Appearing in my thoughts, which I can't seem to
ignore.

The nights grow long as the screen glows bright,
Your words like whispers in the still of night.
"Are you there?" and the ping feels like fate,
Staring at my screen, hoping to see you, has
been worth the wait!

Your laugh, a lifeline through the phone,
Though the distance reminds me I'm still alone.
I trace your voice in my mind's quiet space,
A thousand miles can't erase your face.

Yahoo chats where love confesses,
In clumsy words and nervous guesses.
Hotmail letters, treasures I keep,
Reread at dawn when I cannot sleep.

My chest is full, yet it's hollow too,
Half with me, half with you.
Aching joy, bittersweet and true,
To love someone I can't run to.

Will this endure, our relationship so pure,
The longing hurts, but it means so much.
For now, I hold the connection tight,
Dreaming of you beneath the same starlight!

The Silence Between Us

Once, words flowed like rivers untamed,
Now, the silence lingers, heavy and unnamed.
Each message sent feels like a plea,
A fragile paper boat lost at sea.

I wait for the chime, the blinking light,
But nothing comes—not day, not night.
The yawning gap where your voice once stayed,
Grows deeper with every word delayed.

Did I say too much, or not enough?
Was love supposed to be this tough?
I replay moments, searching for clues,
Piecing together the "me" I might lose.

Your absence is louder than any goodbye,
An echoing void where dreams used to lie.
I write you letters you'll never read,
Pouring my heart where it can't be freed.

The ache is sharp, like a phantom limb,
Reaching for you in shadows dim.
But the tether is frayed, the line is cold,
And I'm left with stories we'll never retold.

So here I stand, with a heart that's torn,
Learning to mourn what was never born.
Goodbye, my love, though you never said,
Your silence speaks what my soul has read.

The Lies

This was a time when I felt abandoned, lost,
unworthy.
I kept asking myself, why? Why me?

A phase of self-doubt and seeking empathy. I
turned to my friends,
Hoping they could put an end to this agony.

I met people who came across as my
well-wishers,
Who saw the good in me and made me feel
worthy again.

So, I chose to lie, to please, to let them stay and
not leave.
I lied to hide the void within me,
Still yearning for a love that wasn't mine. I lied
to fit into the norms they created for me.
I lied to myself, believing this love was for me.

The Wake-up Call

"What were you thinking?"
"We need to work on your dressing."
"Do you even know this... hahaha... you're too
naive."
"You can't do this."
"Who is this guy?"
"Why aren't you picking up my calls?"

When this became routine,
The questions and explanations,
The arguments and defenses,
I started to wonder—was it just me?

I began doubting if all this was true.
I was messing up by being dumb.
It was me again, the one!
All those lies were catching up soon,
And I finally had a wake-up call, an afternoon.

He glorified a character from a movie,
And in the process, questioned mine. It pierced
through my heart…
He sure was an ace archer.

Why do I need to explain myself?
Why do I need to report myself, like I've
committed a crime?

Do I want to live in these chains, under the name
of love,
With someone who will always think he's way
up above?

That was the day I decided to break these chains
and face my fear,
The day I chose to never let myself succumb to
helpless tears.

A New Dawn

A fresh start in a small town,
Where quiet hills and empty roads drown
The noise of the past, the cries of old,
Yet in my heart, a story still unfolds.

I moved here to find some peace,
But guilt lingers, a never-ending lease.
I let distractions steal my time,
Now I'm chasing a rhythm, trying to climb.

I focus on family, the love they give,
In their smiles, I learn to forgive.
My books are open, the pages turn,
In every lesson, a chance to return.

But my thoughts still wander back to you,
To the love I lost, the dreams we knew.
Do you still think of me in the quiet night?
Or has the echo of my name faded from sight?

The pain of what was, what never could be,
It tags along, like a shadow following me.
I wonder if it's a wound that will ever heal,
Or just a scar, a past I can't conceal.

But I take each step with hope anew,
Focusing on what's here, not on what's through.
For in the stillness, I find my way,
As the sun rises on a brighter day.

New Beginnings

It was time to move again,
To an unknown city with a bucket full of guilt.
I had let down my parents,
I had within me, a lot of regrets!

I decided it was time to fix it,
But my heart was still aching,
Still wondering if he would reach out to me, or
am I history again?
I spent nights crying silently, praying to God to
relieve me of this pain!

It was time to step out,
Start my life afresh.
Leaving behind what dragged me down,
I finally agreed to the advice which seemed
sound.
Bidding this sleepy town adieu,
I decided to move on and live my life again, it
was due!

Hatching Out of My Cocoon

I landed with eyes all dreamy,
Waiting to see what this world had to offer me.
Finally, I felt I'd done something right,
My parents' pride shining bright.

A bit scared to be left alone,
I tried to figure out how to survive on my own.
Being with Mom had felt so special,
The thought of leaving her felt so real and
crucial.

Seeing her off, I realized this was it,
It was time to step forward, to make my fit.
Hoping for a new chapter to unfold,
I put on a brave face, though my heart was still
bold.

I didn't know yet what it meant to be brave,
But I was ready to take what life gave.

Learning to Fly

I was a new bee, learning to spread my wings,
Excited to break free from all those old-school
things.

I believed in myself, thought I deserved this
success,
I'd worked hard to rise, pulling myself from the
mess.

Starting over had become my way,
Every time I got a chance, I'd grab it, come what
may.
To be a new version, a wiser me—
But was I truly that, or just pretending to be?

I was still a girl, craving validation,
Seeking it in any form, in any station.
Confused about my aspirations, deep inside,
Wondering if I was right, or just taking things in
stride.

Was I enough, or did I need fixing to fit the
mold?
The past kept pulling me back, its grip strong
and bold,
While I was ready to spread my wings, take
flight,
To leave behind the shadows and step into the
light.

Losing My Way

Attention can be addictive,
When suddenly you're in the spotlight for the
way you look!
It feels like a scene straight out of the movies,
The world eager to join your troupe, your book.

It felt good to see people fight over me;
In that moment, I thought it soothed my soul.
Comforted by the thought, "Hey, you're
enough,"
No doubts, no flaws, it made me feel whole.

Joining the parties, dancing my sorrows away,
Laughing, pretending I've always been this way.
Soaked in naivety, blinded by lies,
I was flying high, falling through the skies.

Being "Labelled"

The kind of girl who laughs with boys,
The kind who talks to them,
Or the kind who gets too candid about her
past—
You know, that "kind of a girl"!

The labels I wore while just trying to be me,
Trying to explore, not caring how they would
see.
I should have, perhaps, thought about this a bit,
Maybe, I could've saved my soul from a few
more hits.

Who am I? A slut, a whore, an easy chick to use
and toss.
These were the thoughts that began to emboss,
Filling my mind with endless labels,
Digging at my soul with rusted, cruel shovels.

Rescuing Myself

We're often conditioned to believe
That we need someone to come and save us,
A helping hand, most likely a man,
To rescue us from all our pain.

But think about it—how often has a man
Given you pain, rather than saving you from it?
So why wait, in vain, for a rescue that won't fit?

It's always been you, yourself, who holds the
power,
To let go of the things that drain you, hour by
hour,
And wash them away in a cleansing shower.

It was this truth that set me free,
From the game of love and hate, taking flight.
As long as I loved myself,
The world's opinion would lose its bite.

Taking Flight

Time flew at its pace,
There were days when you wanted it to go slow,
And then the others which just dragged on and
on.
Most days, I was lost in space,
Listening to my then-favorite songs!

The day was here, for which everyone was
excited,
A day that decided our worth,
Skill, talent, knowledge, all of it on display,
There was absolutely no dearth.

People placed bets on their favorites and the
losers,
And my name was on the right side more often
than I would like.

Nervous and ashamed, I was scared to even
apply.
But a friend called, and thank God she did,
To wake me up from my slumber and come and
grab a number.

Round after round, I hoped to move forward,
And the moment I did, it seemed like some
miracle showered.

Finally, when I had the letter in hand, so proud,
It felt like an answer to all those doubts, making
me stand apart from the crowd!

The win was mine,
And I would like to believe I fought a fair case.
It gave me a strange pleasure when I saw the
disappointment on a certain face.
It was time for me to take off,
As I wind up, after winning this race!

Adulting

Living on your own is no joke,
Nor is it as magical as the TV folks invoke.
It brings a sense of freedom, a powerful kick,
But it also has its downsides, which no one will pick.

With each passing day, I missed "Home" the most,
The love, the care, the warm hugs, the food—
And my people, scattered and far,
While I stood here, trying to heal the scars.

I couldn't let them see how scared I was,
How lonely I felt in this bustling new city,
Surrounded by people, but none of my own,
Trying to stand tall, yet feeling unknown!

Setting Up My Nest

I finally found a place I could call "Home,"
A place that felt just right,
With big windows and a balcony,
Overlooking the river's gentle light.

It felt safe here,
Like a space I had known forever.
Strange how some places can make you feel
different,
This one soothed my soul,
Making it my haven—
A corner where I could unfold.

This was my nest, for now,
A place that gave me a sense of belonging,
Helping me accept this city, bit by bit,
Coping with loneliness and all the love I was
longing.

Mom…

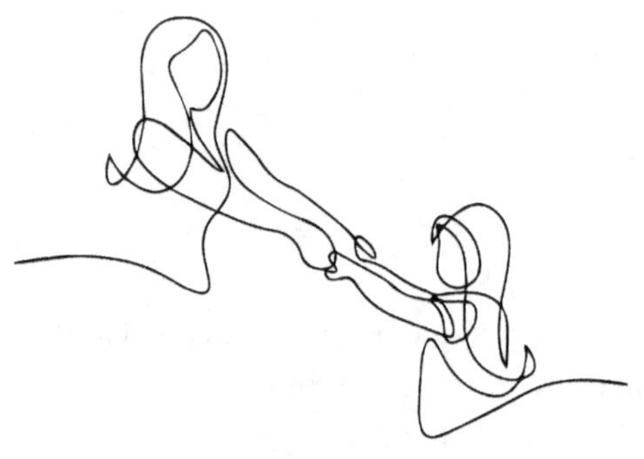

My mom was about to visit me,
And I couldn't wait, making sure my place was neat,
The lights just right, every corner set,
Hoping everything would be perfect when we met.

It felt strange to make arrangements for Mom,
As she was always the one handling it back home.
The day arrived, and tears began to fall,
Seeing her walk towards me, I felt my world stand tall—
She was my sun, my light, returning to me.

What I missed most was sharing that cup of tea,
Talking about our day, laughing at what we'd
see.
The warmth of having her close,
I longed to make every minute with her count
the most.

And in that moment, as time seemed to slow,
I realized how much I had missed her love, her
glow.
The simple things that once felt routine,
Now felt like treasures, more precious than
they'd ever been.
I knew this visit would be a memory to keep,
A reminder that no matter the distance, love runs
deep.

And it Rained

I woke to the soothing scent of wet earth,
A quiet invitation to pause and reflect.
"Why not take a day off?" I thought to myself,
Let the world spin on while I connect.

The rain whispered a calming song,
As it kissed the earth and sang along.
Shiny leaves glistened, flowers bloomed,
And in the cool breeze, my heart was groomed.

We rush through life, forgetting to breathe,
Missing nature's touch that helps us believe—
That in the rain's soft embrace,
Our restless souls find their place.

It's a balm for the heart, a healing reprieve,
A sacred pause, where we can just be.

Learning to Love Myself First…

Love is often seen as a gift for others,
A treasure to be kept safe from evil eyes,
But why do we forget to love ourselves first,
To be kind, compassionate, and wise?

Why is it so hard to be content on our own?
Why do we crave company, even at the cost of
losing our own tone?
These questions kept me awake, making me
wonder,
And pushed me to step out, breaking the
thunder.

I began to embrace my true self,
Slowly, steadily, like pulling a book off the
shelf.
And as I did, the glow started to show—
The love I'd been missing began to flow.

Thank You for Standing by Me...

It was a difficult phase back then,
When my mind was far from being Zen.
I'd cried so much,
Over a relationship I knew was losing touch.

I desperately needed to see my girl,
Who was fighting demons of her own,
Together we'd sailed through storms so wild,
Swimming through tides that could've torn us
apart for a while.

So I took the flight, reached out to her,
She took my hand, offered me her shoulder,
To soak up the pain, wash it all away,
To speak the words I'd been too scared to say.

In times like these, you realize—
It's your girls who truly stand by,
Who see you for who you are,
And remind you to never lower the bar.

The Act of Letting Go...

Once you wake up to reality,
And see how a relationship truly makes you feel,
It's time to think, to pause,
And decide if you want to heal.

You can stay and feel empty,
Or break those chains and set yourself free,
There's joy to be found, waiting for you,
A life where you can simply be.

Being together is sacred when it's right,
It should never be an excuse to make one
another feel light.
To treat someone as a slave,
Or make them feel worthless, just to behave.

Respect the boundaries, never break them,
Trust your partner, and let them live.
Let them explore life on their own terms,
Without turning love into something to resent or
burn.

The Spark in ME!

Shedding the layers that held me tight,
I searched for the spark that once felt right.
I wavered from my goals,
Choking my soul with every toll.

The pain that lingered, never letting go,
Had become part of me, in ways I didn't know.
But one day, I chose to be free,
Done with the life of agony,
I confronted my fears, standing tall,
Ready to face whatever came to call.

It wasn't an enemy, not one outside—
But the norms that kept me tied,
To please everyone, to hide my pain,
Even when it crumbled my pride, again and
again.

To be free, I had to be me,
True, authentic, and wild with possibility.
Breaking those chains has not been easy,
But in the struggle, I found the spark that was
always within me.